Heaven's
BIG
Secret

HEAVEN'S BIG SECRET

THE EASTER STORY

WRITTEN BY
KAREN LANGTREE

spck

ILLUSTRATED BY
NATALIA MOORE

Something was happening in heaven.

Alfie and Alia, two of the smallest
angels, listened carefully.
What were the big angels
whispering about?

Alia made a plan. 'Let's fly down to Earth and find out!'

When they arrived, they spied a donkey, preparing for a special journey.

'What's going on?' asked Alfie.

'**Hee-haw!**' the donkey said. 'I've been chosen to carry Jesus into Jerusalem. Fancy that! The King, on my back!'

'We must follow,' Alia said.

As the donkey strode through the streets, the crowds cheered.

'Hooray for King Jesus!'

'Hosanna!'

'Aha! This must be what they were whispering about in heaven!' said Alfie.

But, Alia noticed some people with grumpy faces, huddled together.

'Grumble!'
'Rumble!' 'Mumble!'
'Scumble!'

'I wonder what they're grumbling about?' she thought.

Later on, Alfie and Alia arrived at a house where Jesus had prepared a special meal for his friends.

At the table, Jesus passed a cup of wine around and shared some bread. Crumbs showered the floor, and Alfie noticed a mischievous mouse greedily gobbling them up.

'What's going on?' asked Alfie.

'Jesus is saying goodbye,' said the mouse.

'Where's he going?' asked Alia. The mouse just kept on munching.

Jesus and his friends got up to leave.

'We must follow,'
said Alia.

A stream of silver moonlight swept along the path. The angels followed as Jesus led the way to a garden and asked his friends to pray with him. But . . .

YAWN

One by one, they fell asleep, until only Jesus was awake.

'He's very upset,' Alia whispered.

'What should we do?' asked Alfie.

It was true! Jesus' friends had run away.
'**Help!**' cried the angels, but there was no one left to hear them.

'We must follow,' whispered Alia.

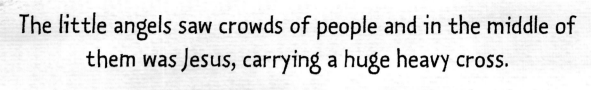

The little angels saw crowds of people and in the middle of them was Jesus, carrying a huge heavy cross.

But this time, the people were not shouting 'Hosanna'. They were shouting for Jesus to be killed!

'I can't watch,' said Alia, covering her face.

'We must follow,' said Alfie.

Later, the two little angels sat together on a hillside. Alia had her wing around Alfie. A snowy white dove fluttered down, cooing a soft sad song.
'Coo-coo. Coo-coo.'

The sound was soothing. 'Do *you* know what's going on?' asked Alfie.

The dove cooed, **'Looook! Looook!'**

Three dark crosses stood on a hill in the distance.
The dove told them that Jesus had died on one of them.

'So that's why he was saying goodbye,' said Alia.

Alfie nodded. 'Maybe *that* is what they were whispering about in heaven.'

As the sun was setting, Alfie and Alia found the donkey,
pulling a cart with a heavy load.
People followed, crying.

'What's going on?' asked Alfie.

'I'm taking Jesus' body to be laid in a tomb,'
said the donkey.

Alfie and Alia joined the procession and
watched as Jesus was laid in the tomb.

A heavy rock was rolled across the entrance.

The angels tried to keep watch, but they were *so* tired.

Early on Sunday morning, Alfie opened his eyes. He gasped!
The rock had been rolled away! How had that happened?

'Alia! Wake up! Look!'

Alia looked up sleepily and stared at the tomb,
her eyes wide. 'Let's look inside.'

It was dark in the cave, but a shaft of sunlight streamed through the entrance like a spotlight. Jesus' body had disappeared!

'Has someone taken him?' asked Alfie.

'Or has he escaped?' suggested Alia.

Alfie shook his head. 'How could he? He's . . .'

Just then, they heard a noise.

Nervously, they peered out of the cave.

There sat Mary, one of Jesus' friends. She was crying. A man sat down beside her and she asked him if he had taken Jesus away.

The man said one word: **'Mary.'**

Mary's eyes lit up. The little angels recognized that voice!

'It's Jesus!' exclaimed Alfie.

Alia beamed. 'He's alive! He's risen from the dead!'

'So, *that's* what they were whispering about in heaven!'
Alia said. 'It turned out to be good news.'

The little angels were so happy that they gathered all their animal friends.
Alfie announced, 'Jesus is alive! He's brought new life for everyone!'

'**Hooray!**' they all shouted.
'That really *is* good news!'

First published in Great Britain in 2020

Society for Promoting Christian Knowledge
36 Causton Street
London SW1P 4ST
www.spck.org.uk

British Library Cataloguing-in-Publication Data
A catalogue record for this book is available from the British Library

ISBN 978–0–281–07730–4

Typeset and designed by Chris Fraser
Printed by Imago
Subsequently digitally printed in Great Britain

Produced on paper from sustainable forests